The Stars About Love

Mrigendra Bharti

Published by Sellbrochure Vymish Entertainment, 2024.

THE STARS ABOUT LOVE

First edition. July 4, 2024.

Copyright © 2024 Mrigendra Bharti.

ISBN: 979-8227626592

Written by Mrigendra Bharti.

Preface

In the vast expanse of the cosmos, amidst the twinkling stars and celestial wonders, lies a timeless tale – the story of love. For centuries, humanity has found solace, inspiration, and a deep sense of connection in the starry skies, believing that these celestial bodies hold the secrets to the universe's most profound emotion.

This book, "The Stars About Love," is a tribute to this enduring connection. It is a collection of poems that weave together the themes of love, loss, longing, and hope, all set against the backdrop of the starlit heavens.

As you delve into these pages, you will encounter a myriad of emotions, from the tender whispers of first love to the bittersweet pangs of heartbreak. You will meet star-crossed lovers, celestial deities, and everyday individuals who find solace and wonder in the starry expanse.

Each poem is a brushstroke in a grand cosmic painting, capturing the essence of love in its myriad forms. The stars, like celestial guides, illuminate our path, reminding us that even in the darkest of nights, love's light can always be found.

Prepare to embark on a romantic journey through the cosmos, where the stars themselves become our guiding light. As you turn the pages, may you find your own love story reflected in the vast and luminous tapestry of the night sky.

 MRIGENDRA BHARTI

This preface introduces the book's theme of love under the stars and sets the tone for the collection of poems. It also highlights the different emotions that will be explored in the poems, from joy to sorrow, and emphasizes the role of stars as celestial guides and symbols of love.

Prologue

In the hush of a twilight fading, the sun dipped below the horizon, painting the sky with hues of fiery orange and bruised purple. A gentle breeze whispered through the trees, carrying the scent of damp earth and the promise of a cool night. Beneath the deepening indigo canvas, a million pinpricks of light began to emerge, one by one, like scattered diamonds on black velvet.

Tonight, the world held its breath. Anticipation crackled in the air, a silent symphony waiting to be played. For tonight, the stories whispered on the wind, the secrets carried by the constellations, and the desires etched in the hearts of lovers would all find their voice under the watchful gaze of the stars.

Here, in this timeless dance between celestial light and earthly passion, we begin our journey. We will meet those who seek solace in the starry expanse, those who search for answers in the celestial tapestry, and those who find their love stories written amongst the twinkling diamonds above.

Prepare to be swept away on a cosmic adventure, where whispers of love mingle with the stardust, and the vastness of the universe becomes a canvas for the human heart. Open your eyes, open your ears, and open your soul. Let the stars be your guide, and allow the poems within to paint a picture of love's eternal dance under the celestial dome.

Acknowledgment

These poems are a tribute to a special someone who has touched my heart in ways I never thought possible. While I choose not to reveal their name, their presence in my life has been a source of endless inspiration and joy.

To my muse, my guiding star, my beacon of light – these poems are for you. Thank you for being the embodiment of love, beauty, and grace. Your unwavering support and encouragement have been the driving force behind my creative journey.

I hope these poems capture a glimpse of the admiration and affection I hold for you. You are the reason my heart sings, and I am forever grateful for the impact you have had on my life.

With all my love and gratitude,

Mrigendra Bharti

About Sellbrochure Vymish Entertainment

Sellbrochure Vymish Entertainment, recognized as India's largest book publishing company, has made significant strides in ensuring its extensive collection of books reaches audiences across the global market. This rapid expansion is a testament to the company's dedication to disseminating knowledge and literature far beyond national borders. Central to its success is its affiliation with InkWhirl Media Networks, a reputable entity in the media and publication industry known for its innovative and strategic approaches. Within this network, InkWhirl Publication LLC operates as a vital division, further enhancing the company's capabilities and reach in the international market. The visionary behind this enterprise is Mrigendra Bharti, the founder of Sellbrochure Vymish Entertainment. His foresight and passion for the literary world have been instrumental in steering the company towards remarkable growth and recognition. Under his leadership, Sellbrochure Vymish Entertainment has not only expanded its catalog but also established a strong presence in both domestic and international markets. Mrigendra Bharti's commitment to excellence and innovation has been a driving force in the company's journey, ensuring that it stays ahead of industry trends and meets the evolving needs of readers worldwide.

Sellbrochure Vymish Entertainment operates under the robust support of its parental organization, Mrigendra Bharti Group InfoTech. This affiliation provides the necessary resources and strategic guidance, enabling the publishing company to undertake ambitious projects and explore new markets. Mrigendra Bharti Group InfoTech's extensive experience in technology and information services has been a valuable asset, allowing Sellbrochure Vymish Entertainment to integrate advanced digital solutions in its operations, thereby enhancing its distribution capabilities and reader engagement.

Through relentless efforts and a commitment to quality, Sellbrochure Vymish Entertainment continues to break barriers and expand the reach of Indian literature globally. The company's diverse portfolio includes a wide range of genres, catering to different age groups and interests, thereby fostering a rich and inclusive reading culture. As it continues to innovate and grow, Sellbrochure Vymish Entertainment remains dedicated to its mission of making literature accessible to all, contributing significantly to the global literary landscape.

Connect With Mrigendra,
Thank you very much for choosing this book.
You can also connect with me on Instagram,
https://www.instagram.com/i_mrigendrabharti.official
With Love,
Mrigendra Bharti

Introduction

Have you ever gazed upon the night sky and felt a connection so profound it left you breathless? For centuries, lovers have sought solace, inspiration, and a deeper understanding of love in the celestial dance of stars. This book, "The Stars About Love," is an invitation to embark on a romantic journey through the cosmos, where the stardust whispers secrets and the vast expanse becomes a canvas for the human heart.

Within these pages, you'll encounter a collection of poems penned beneath the watchful gaze of the stars. Each poem is a brushstroke in a grand cosmic painting, capturing the essence of love in its myriad forms.

* Yearning and Longing: We'll explore the bittersweet pangs of unrequited love, the whispers of longing on a starry night, and the yearning for a love that feels destined.

* Passion and Desire: The poems will ignite with the heat of passionate love, the thrill of stolen glances under the celestial dome, and the promises whispered against a backdrop of twinkling stars.

* Comfort and Solace: We'll find solace in the quiet companionship of the stars, the sense of peace that washes over us beneath a starlit sky, and the enduring strength love offers in times of darkness.

* Growth and Transformation: The poems will explore how love, like the constellations, can shift and change over time, revealing new depths and dimensions as our journeys unfold.

As you turn the pages, allow yourself to be swept away by the celestial symphony of love and light. Perhaps you'll find echoes of your own love story reflected in the stardust, or maybe you'll discover a new facet of love's beauty through the lens of these poems.

Starry Rendezvous

In velvet skies, where stars ignite,
Our hearts entwined, bathed in soft light.
Beneath the moon's ethereal glow,
Our love's embrace, a cosmic show.
The heavens dance, a symphony of light,
Reflecting passions, burning ever so bright.
In constellations, our love takes form,
An eternal bond, defying life's storm.
Amidst the cosmos, our souls align,
Two hearts as one, forever to shine.
In starry whispers, love's secrets unfold,
A tale of devotion, forever to be told.

Celestial Sonnet

Oh, stars above, bear witness to our plight,
Two souls entwined, bathed in moon's soft light.
In your celestial tapestry, our love's design,
A cosmic dance, where hearts entwine.
Like constellations etched in starry skies,
Our love endures, defying time's disguise.
Through cosmic cycles, our bond remains,
An eternal flame, untouched by earthly stains.
The universe, our witness, vast and grand,
As love's symphony plays across the land.
In starry whispers, our hearts converse,
A love so pure, it transcends the universe.

Love's Cosmic Tapestry

In starlit skies, our love's story unfolds,
A tapestry of dreams, in starlight it molds.
Each twinkling gem, a symbol of our plight,
Two souls entwined, bathed in celestial light.
The moon, a beacon, guiding our way,
As through the cosmos, our love holds sway.
In constellations, our destiny we trace,
A love so profound, it spans time and space.
The stars above, our silent confidantes,
As in their embrace, our love expands.
A cosmic dance, where hearts align,
In love's embrace, forever to shine.

Love's Stellar Symphony

In starry skies, a symphony ignites,
As love's sweet melody takes flight.
The stars, our orchestra, in harmony they play,
A cosmic serenade, to guide our way.
Each note a whisper, of love's tender touch,
A symphony of emotions, oh, so much.
The universe, our concert hall so grand,
Where love's sweet music fills the land.
In starry rhythms, our hearts beat as one,
A love so pure, it has just begun.
The stars above, our eternal choir,
As love's symphony plays forever higher.

Whispers in the Milky Way

The Milky Way, a river of light,
Whispers secrets of love in the night.
Lost in its embrace, we wander and stray,
Two souls entwined, forever we'll stay.
Diamonds scattered across the inky black,
Reflect the love that brings us back.
In stardust dreams, our futures unfold,
A love story whispered, never to be old.
Beneath the celestial canopy vast,
Our love's a promise, forever to last.
With every twinkle, a wish takes flight,
Forever tethered, by love's gentle light.

A Shooting Star's Promise

A streak of fire, a fleeting sight,
A shooting star, on this starry night.
A wish I whisper, with all my might,
To love you forever, bathed in moonlight.
The heavens sigh, a silent decree,
Our love's destiny, for all to see.
Written in stardust, a love so true,
A promise whispered, just me and you.
The stars above, our silent vow,
A love that burns ever so bright, somehow.
In celestial whispers, our feelings ignite,
Two hearts forever, bathed in starry light.

Moonlit Serenade

Beneath the moon's soft, silvery glow,
A love song plays, a gentle flow.
The crickets chirp, a sweet serenade,
As in your arms, my love is displayed.
The stars peek down, like celestial eyes,
Witnessing love that never dies.
In this cosmic dance, we sway and spin,
Two souls connected, where love's fire begins.
The universe conspires, to make us complete,
A love story whispered, forever so sweet.
With every heartbeat, our love takes flight,
Under the moonlit sky, bathed in gentle light.

Constellation of Two

In the vast expanse, where stars ignite,
We forge our own constellation, bathed in moonlight.
Two hearts entwined, a celestial bind,
A love story written, for all humankind.
The Big Dipper watches, with wisdom untold,
As our love unfolds, braver and bold.
The Milky Way shimmers, a celestial stream,
Reflecting the passion, in our love's dream.
Forever etched in the starry display,
A love that burns brighter, with each passing day.
Two souls destined, to forever combine,
A constellation of love, forever to shine.

Starry Sanctuary

Beneath the velvet cloak of night,
A million stars, a dazzling sight.
We seek refuge, in this starry space,
Two souls entwined, in love's embrace.
The moonbeams paint a silvery sheen,
On a love story, eternally serene.
Whispers of passion, on the cosmic breeze,
Lost in a world, where only love appease.
The constellations, our silent guides,
As love's tender flame, forever confides.
In this starry sanctuary, we find our peace,
A love everlasting, with never a cease.

Symphony of Starlight

The heavens erupt, in a symphony grand,
A million stars, playing at your command.
A celestial concerto, of love's sweet refrain,
A melody echoing, washing away pain.
The shooting stars, like fireflies alight,
Illuminate our path, through the darkest night.
In this cosmic dance, our hearts take flight,
Soaring high above, bathed in starry light.
The universe conspires, to make our love complete,
A love song whispered, forever so sweet.
With every twinkling beat, our souls entwine,
A symphony of starlight, forever divine.

Coalescence Under the Stars

Like distant galaxies, once we were apart,
But fate intervened, a celestial spark.
Drawn together, by an invisible force,
Our destinies entwined, on an infinite course.
Beneath the watchful gaze of the Milky Way,
Our hearts collide, in a brilliant display.
Two souls merging, a beautiful sight,
A love story written, in stardust's light.
The stars above, our silent applause,
As we become one, forever because.
In this cosmic ballet, we gracefully bend,
Two souls united, until the very end.

Starry-Eyed Vows

With stars as our witnesses, we pledge our vow,
A love everlasting, here and now.
The moon, a beacon, bathes us in its glow,
As promises whispered, forever flow.
The constellations, guardians of time,
Etch our love story, in verse sublime.
Hand in hand, beneath the starry dome,
We weave a future, forever to call home.
The universe listens, to our heartfelt plea,
A love so boundless, flowing eternally.
In this starry sanctuary, our souls take flight,
Bound by love's promise, bathed in starry light.

Celestial Lullaby

Beneath a canopy of stardust bright,
We drift to sleep, in the moon's soft light.
The celestial hush, a gentle refrain,
A lullaby whispered, easing away pain.
The stars above, like diamonds they gleam,
Guarding our dreams, a celestial team.
In whispered constellations, our love takes flight,
A promise of forever, bathed in starry night.
With each lullaby note, the universe conspires,
To fill our hearts with love's gentle fires.
As eyelids flutter, and dreams begin to unfold,
Our love's embrace keeps us warm, from the night's gentle cold.

Starlit Secrets

Under the cloak of a star-studded sky,
Secrets of the heart, we don't deny.
Whispers of love, on the cosmic breeze,
Two souls entwined, with hearts at ease.
The moon, a confidante, with a knowing smile,
Listens to our stories, for a long, long while.
The constellations, like celestial eyes,
Reflect the emotions, that in our hearts lie.
In this starry haven, our vulnerabilities blend,
A love story whispered, with no need to pretend.
Forever etched in the stardust's embrace,
Secrets of the heart, find their rightful place.

A Starry Tryst

The night unfolds, a celestial scene,
As we meet beneath the stars, bathed in their sheen.
A stolen moment, a lover's tryst,
Under the watchful gaze, of the moon's gentle mist.
The fireflies dance, like twinkling light,
Guiding our way, through the starlit night.
The scent of jasmine fills the air,
As love's tender whispers, fill the atmosphere.
Time stands still, in this cosmic embrace,
A love story written, on love's gentle face.
With every stolen kiss, beneath the starry dome,
Our love ignites brighter, forever to call home.

Starry-Eyed Dreams

With eyes fixed on the heavens above,
We dream of a future, filled with endless love.
The stars, like celestial guiding lights,
Lead us on a path, forever bright.
The Milky Way shimmers, a river of dreams,
Reflecting the passion, that brightly beams.
In whispered constellations, our hopes unfold,
A love story written, in stardust of gold.
Hand in hand, beneath the starry display,
We chase our dreams, each and every day.
Forever bound, by love's gentle hold,
Our starry-eyed dreams, forever unfold.

Moondust Sonata

Beneath a canvas of celestial grace,
We sway in a dance, a moonlit embrace.
The stars compose a symphony so grand,
A moondust sonata, played by love's hand.
The Milky Way shimmers, a luminous stream,
Reflecting the passion in our love's dream.
With every twinkling note, our souls take flight,
Lost in a melody, bathed in starry light.
The universe whispers secrets in the breeze,
A love story written, for all the world to see.
In this cosmic waltz, forever we'll entwine,
Two hearts as one, beneath the moon's gentle shine.

Stardust Memoirs

Under a tapestry of stardust so bright,
We weave our memoirs, bathed in moon's soft light.
The constellations, like ancestral lore,
Guide us on our journey, forevermore.
The shooting stars, like wishes alight,
Carry our dreams, soaring through the night.
In whispered stories, etched in starry rhyme,
Our love's legacy transcends the sands of time.
Forever bound by this celestial vow,
Our love story unfolds, here and now.
With every stardust memory, love's embers glow,
A testament to our bond, that forever will grow.

Celestial Rendezvous

A million stars ignite the velvet night,
As we meet again, bathed in moon's gentle light.
A celestial rendezvous, hearts ablaze,
Reaffirming our love, in a myriad of ways.
The Milky Way whispers secrets untold,
Of a love story, braver and bold.
The constellations, like celestial sparks,
Reflect the passion that forever embarks.
In this starry haven, our souls collide,
Two hearts entwined, with love as our guide.
A timeless connection, forever defined,
By this celestial rendezvous, forever enshrined.

Starry-Eyed Escape

Beneath a canopy of celestial might,
We seek solace, bathed in moon's gentle light.
The stars, our companions, on this starry flight,
A refuge from worries, a world so bright.
The fireflies twinkle, like celestial fire,
Guiding our way, fueled by love's desire.
Lost in this sanctuary, vast and deep,
Our worries fade away, as we peacefully sleep.
The universe conspires, to set our hearts free,
In this starry-eyed escape, eternally.
With each breath we take, beneath the starry dome,
Love's embrace enfolds us, forever our home.

Cosmic Lullaby

As slumber descends on the starry expanse,
A cosmic lullaby graces our trance.
The crickets chirp, a gentle refrain,
Lulling us softly, washing away pain.
The moonbeams cascade, a silvery stream,
Guiding our dreams, a celestial dream.
In constellations, our love takes flight,
A promise of forever, bathed in starry light.
With each twinkling beat, the universe sighs,
Filling our hearts with love's gentle ties.
Wrapped in stardust's embrace, we drift away,
Two souls entwined, until the break of day.

Starlight Sonata

Beneath a canopy of celestial grace,
We move in a dance, a love's embrace.
The stars compose a symphony so grand,
A starlight sonata, played by love's hand.
The Milky Way shimmers, a luminous stream,
Reflecting the passion in our love's dream.
With every twinkling note, our souls entwine,
Lost in a melody, forever divine.
The universe whispers secrets in the breeze,
A love story written, for all the world to appease.
In this cosmic waltz, forever we'll combine,
Two hearts as one, beneath the starlight's shine.

Celestial Canvas

The heavens unfold, a majestic display,
A canvas splashed with stars, lighting our way.
The moon, a spotlight, casts a silvery gleam,
On a love story painted, in a celestial dream.
The constellations, like brushstrokes so bright,
Outline our future, bathed in moon's soft light.
Shooting stars streak by, wishes alight,
Promises whispered, on this starry night.
Forever etched in this celestial art,
Two souls entwined, a love that takes part.
In this masterpiece of stardust's embrace,
Our love story unfolds, leaving its trace.

Starry-Eyed Vows

With stars as our witnesses, we pledge our vow,
A love everlasting, under the heavens now.
The moonbeams dance, a celestial show,
As promises whispered, forever flow.
The constellations, like guardians wise,
Etch our love story, in starry skies.
Hand in hand, beneath the starry dome,
We weave a future, forever our home.
The universe listens, to our heartfelt plea,
A love so boundless, flowing eternally.
In this starry sanctuary, our souls take flight,
Bound by love's promise, bathed in starry light.

Whispers in the Milky Way

The Milky Way, a celestial stream,
Whispers secrets of love in a starry dream.
Lost in its embrace, we wander and roam,
Two souls entwined, forever to call home.
Diamonds scattered across the velvet night,
Reflect the love that burns ever so bright.
In stardust dreams, our futures unfold,
A love story whispered, never to grow old.
Beneath the celestial canopy vast,
Our love's a promise, forever to last.
With every twinkle, a wish takes flight,
Forever tethered, by love's gentle light.

A Shooting Star's Promise

A streak of fire, a fleeting sight,
A shooting star on this magical night.
A wish I whisper, with all my might,
To love you forever, bathed in moonlight.
The heavens sigh, a silent decree,
Our love's destiny, for all to see.
Written in stardust, a love so true,
A promise whispered, just me and you.
The stars above, our silent vow,
A love that burns ever so bright, somehow.
In celestial whispers, our feelings ignite,
Two hearts forever, bathed in starry light.

Moonlit Serenade

Beneath the moon's soft, silvery glow,
A love song plays, a gentle flow.
The crickets chirp, a sweet serenade,
As in your arms, my love is displayed.
The stars peek down, like celestial eyes,
Witnessing love that never dies.
In this cosmic dance, we sway and spin,
Two souls connected, where love's fire begins.
The universe conspires, to make us complete,
A love story whispered, forever so sweet.
With every heartbeat, our love takes flight,
Under the moonlit sky, bathed in gentle light.

Constellation of Two

In the vast expanse, where stars ignite,
We forge our own constellation, bathed in moonlight.
Two hearts entwined, a celestial bind,
A love story written, for all humankind.
The Big Dipper watches, with wisdom untold,
As our love unfolds, braver and bold.
The Milky Way shimmers, a celestial stream,
Reflecting the passion, in our love's dream.
Forever etched in the starry display,
A love that burns brighter, with each passing day.
Two souls destined, to forever combine,
A constellation of love, forever to shine.

Starry Silhouette

Beneath a canvas of celestial might,
We stand embraced, bathed in moon's soft light.
Our silhouette dances, a love-struck form,
Two souls entwined, safe from life's storm.
The stars peek down, like celestial spies,
Witnessing love reflected in our eyes.
The Milky Way whispers secrets untold,
A love story written, braver and bold.
In this starry sanctuary, we find our peace,
A love everlasting, with never a cease.
Forever etched in this starry frame,
A love so profound, whispered by name.

Celestial Lullaby

As slumber descends on the starry expanse,
A cosmic lullaby graces our trance.
The crickets chirp, a gentle refrain,
Lulling us softly, washing away pain.
The moonbeams cascade, a silvery stream,
Guiding our dreams, a celestial dream.
In constellations, our love takes flight,
A promise of forever, bathed in starry light.
With each twinkling beat, the universe sighs,
Filling our hearts with love's gentle ties.
Wrapped in stardust's embrace, we drift away,
Two souls entwined, until the break of day.

Star-Crossed Symphony

Beneath a canopy of celestial fire,
Our hearts ignite, a love's sweet desire.
The stars above, like musicians grand,
Play a symphony, for our love at hand.
The shooting stars, like celestial sighs,
Echo our passions, reaching for the skies.
The moon conducts, with a silvery gleam,
A love story written, in a celestial dream.
Forever bound by this cosmic refrain,
Two souls entwined, through sunshine and rain.
In this star-crossed symphony, forever we'll stay,
Lost in love's melody, bathed in Milky Way.

Starlight Solace

On nights when shadows lengthen and worries arise,
We seek solace beneath the starlit skies.
The moonbeams bathe us, in a gentle light,
Washing away troubles, setting things right.
The constellations, like celestial friends,
Offer guidance that never ends.
Whispered secrets carried on the breeze,
A love story written, for all the world to appease.
In this starry sanctuary, we find our peace,
A love everlasting, with burdens to release.
Forever held close, by the heavens above,
Our love a beacon, a testament to true love.

Astral Alignment

Beneath a dome of celestial grace,
Our hearts align, in this sacred space.
The stars above, like scattered gems,
Reflect the love within our diadems.
The Milky Way, a shimmering river of light,
Guides our journey, through the darkest night.
Shooting stars streak by, wishes take flight,
Promises whispered, bathed in moon's soft light.
In this cosmic ballet, our souls entwine,
Two destinies merging, forever to shine.
Forever bound by this celestial sign,
A love story written, truly divine.

Stardust Serenade

The heavens erupt, in a symphony grand,
A million stars, playing at your command.
A celestial serenade, of love's sweet refrain,
A melody echoing, washing away pain.
The fireflies flicker, like celestial choirs,
Singing love songs, igniting our desires.
The moon, a spotlight, bathes us in its gleam,
As we sway in a dance, in a starlight dream.
Lost in this moment, forever we'll stay,
Two souls entwined, bathed in Milky Way.
This stardust serenade, forever entwined,
A love story whispered, forever enshrined.

Celestial Canvas

The heavens unfold, a majestic display,
A canvas splashed with stars, lighting our way.
The moon, a brushstroke, paints a silvery gleam,
On a love story painted, in a celestial dream.
The constellations, like constellations so bright,
Outline our future, bathed in moon's soft light.
Shooting stars streak by, wishes take flight,
Promises whispered, on this starry night.
Forever etched in this celestial art,
Two souls entwined, a love that takes part.
In this masterpiece of stardust's embrace,
Our love story unfolds, leaving its trace.

Starry-Eyed Sanctuary

Beneath a cloak of celestial might,
We seek refuge, bathed in moon's gentle light.
The stars, our guardians, forever we see,
A sanctuary of love, eternally.
The crickets chirp, a lullaby so sweet,
As we drift to sleep, emotions complete.
In whispered dreams, on wings of love we soar,
Lost in a universe, where we ask for nothing more.
The constellations watch, with a knowing smile,
As love's embers flicker, for a long, long while.
In this starry haven, our souls take flight,
Forever bound by love's gentle light.

Whispers in the Constellation

Beneath a tapestry of stardust so bright,
We whisper secrets, bathed in moon's soft light.
The constellations, like celestial ears,
Hear our love story, spoken through the years.
The Milky Way shimmers, a river of dreams,
Reflecting the passion, that forever gleams.
In whispered stories, etched in starry rhyme,
Our love's legacy transcends the sands of time.
Forever bound by this celestial vow,
Our love story unfolds, here and now.
With every stardust memory, love's embers glow,
A testament to our bond, that forever will grow.

Starry-Eyed Escape

Beneath a canopy of celestial might,
We seek solace, bathed in moon's gentle light.
The stars, our companions, on this starry flight,
A refuge from worries, a world so bright.
The fireflies twinkle, like celestial fire,
Guiding our way, fueled by love's desire.
Lost in this sanctuary, vast and deep,
Our worries fade away, as we peacefully sleep.
The universe conspires, to set our hearts free,
In this starry-eyed escape, eternally.
With each breath we take, beneath the starry dome,
Love's embrace enfolds us, forever our home.

Cosmic Lullaby

As slumber descends on the starry expanse,
A cosmic lullaby graces our trance.
The crickets chirp, a gentle refrain,
Lulling us softly, washing away pain.
The moonbeams cascade, a silvery stream,
Guiding our dreams, a celestial dream.
In constellations, our love takes flight,
A promise of forever, bathed in starry light.
With each twinkling beat, the universe sighs,
Filling our hearts with love's gentle ties.
Wrapped in stardust's embrace, we drift away,
Two souls entwined, until the break of day.

Starlight Sonata

Beneath a canopy of celestial grace,
We move in a dance, a love's embrace.
The stars compose a symphony so grand,
A starlight sonata, played by love's hand.
The Milky Way shimmers, a luminous stream,
Reflecting the passion in our love's dream.
With every twinkling note, our souls entwine,
Lost in a melody, forever divine.
The universe whispers secrets in the breeze,
A love story written, for all the world to appease.
In this cosmic waltz, forever we'll combine,
Two hearts as one, beneath the starlight's shine.

Celestial Rendezvous

A million stars ignite the velvet night,
As we meet again, bathed in moon's gentle light.
A celestial rendezvous, hearts ablaze,
Reaffirming our love, in a myriad of ways.
The Milky Way whispers secrets untold,
Of a love story, braver and bold.
The constellations, like celestial sparks,
Reflect the passion that forever embarks.
In this starry haven, our souls collide,
Two hearts entwined, with love as our guide.
A timeless connection, forever defined,
By this celestial rendezvous, forever enshrined.

Starry-Eyed Dreams

With eyes fixed on the heavens above,
We dream of a future, filled with endless love.
The stars, like celestial guiding lights,
Lead us on a path, forever bright.
The Milky Way shimmers, a river of dreams,
Reflecting the passion that brightly beams.
In whispered constellations, our hopes unfold,
A love story written, in stardust of gold.
Hand in hand, beneath the starry display,
We chase our dreams, each and every day.
Forever bound by love's gentle hold,
Our starry-eyed dreams, forever unfold.

Stardust Memoirs

Under a tapestry of stardust so bright,
We weave our memoirs, bathed in moon's soft light.
The constellations, like ancestral lore,
Guide us on our journey, forevermore.
The shooting stars, like wishes alight,
Carry our dreams, soaring through the night.
In whispered stories, etched in starry rhyme,
Our love's legacy transcends the sands of time.
Forever bound by this celestial vow,
Our love story unfolds, here and now.
With every stardust memory, love's embers glow,
A testament to our bond, that forever will grow.

A Starry Embrace

Beneath a canvas vast and starlit deep,
We hold each other close, while secrets we keep.
The moon, a confidante, with a gentle sheen,
Bathes us in love's light, a celestial scene.
The stars, like diamonds, scattered and bright,
Reflect the love that burns ever so light.
In whispered promises, our souls entwine,
Forever connected, beneath the divine.
This starry embrace, a haven so true,
Where love's tender whispers forever renew.
Lost in this moment, forever we'll stay,
Held beneath the heavens, bathed in Milky Way.

Celestial Whispers

Beneath a velvet cloak of starlit night,
We stand in wonder, bathed in moon's soft light.
Celestial whispers brush against our ears,
Love's secrets carried on the atmosphere.
The constellations, like celestial guides,
Point towards a future, where our love resides.
Shooting stars streak by, wishes take flight,
Promises whispered, bathed in gentle light.
In this cosmic dance, our hearts find their beat,
Two souls entwined, forever complete.
The universe listens, to our love's decree,
A love story written, for eternity.

Starry-Eyed Vow

With the heavens as our witness, we declare,
A love everlasting, a love beyond compare.
The stars, like diamonds, glitter and gleam,
Reflecting the passion, in our love's dream.
The moonbeams cascade, a silvery stream,
Guiding our journey, bathed in moon's soft beam.
Hand in hand we stand, beneath the starry dome,
Forever bound together, making love our home.
The universe conspires, with a celestial vow,
Two souls destined, to share love here and now.
In this starry sanctuary, our hearts entwine,
Forever connected, beneath the divine.

Stardust Symphony

Beneath a canopy, where stars ignite,
A symphony of love takes flight.
The celestial orchestra, in perfect accord,
Plays a love song, whispered and adored.
The violins sing, a melody so sweet,
Reflecting the passion, where our hearts meet.
The flutes take a breath, a sigh in the breeze,
As love's tender emotions, flow with such ease.
The universe hums, a lullaby of light,
Guiding our souls, through the darkest night.
In this stardust symphony, forever we'll stay,
Lost in love's embrace, bathed in Milky Way.

Celestial Solace

On nights when shadows lengthen and doubt takes hold,
We seek solace beneath the heavens, vast and bold.
The stars, like celestial friends, shimmer bright,
Guiding us onward, through the darkest night.
The moonbeams cascade, a gentle, calming flow,
Washing away worries, helping our spirits grow.
The constellations whisper secrets untold,
A love story written, braver and bold.
In this starry haven, our burdens take flight,
Two souls entwined, bathed in moon's gentle light.
Forever held close, by the heavens above,
Our love a beacon, a testament to true love.

Silent Symphony

Beneath a canvas of celestial grace,
We sit in silence, love in our embrace.
The stars above, like diamonds they gleam,
Reflecting a love, a silent dream.
The crickets chirp, a gentle refrain,
A backdrop for emotions, unspoken, yet plain.
The moon, a gentle spotlight so bright,
Bathes us in its glow, on this starry night.
No words are needed, love speaks in its way,
In whispered glances, hearts forever stay.
In this silent symphony, souls intertwine,
A love story written, truly divine.

Starry-Eyed Discovery

Underneath a tapestry, vast and grand,
We explore the wonders, hand in hand.
The Milky Way, a river of light,
Guiding our journey, through the starry night.
With each constellation, a story unfolds,
Myths and legends, whispered and old.
The shooting stars, like wishes ignite,
Dreams we share, bathed in moon's soft light.
In this celestial classroom, love takes its stand,
Discovery and passion, forever hand in hand.
The universe unfolds, a magical sight,
Our love story written, beneath the starry night.

A Starry Promise

Beneath a sky painted with celestial fire,
A promise we whisper, fueled by love's desire.
The stars as our witness, forever we'll see,
A love story written, eternally.
The moon, a guardian, bathed in gentle light,
Watches over us, as we pledge our might.
To cherish and love, through laughter and tears,
For all of our days, and all of our years.
In this cosmic bond, our fates intertwine,
A love everlasting, forever to shine.
With every twinkling star, the promise takes hold,
A love story whispered, forever to unfold.

Celestial Tapestry

Woven across the night, a tapestry grand,
A million stars, held by love's gentle hand.
The constellations, like threads intertwined,
Reflect the love story, forever enshrined.
The moon, a silver needle, stitching so bright,
Embroiders our future, bathed in moon's soft light.
Shooting stars, like scattered threads of gold,
Dreams and aspirations, forever to be told.
In this celestial masterpiece, love takes its place,
A bond unbreakable, a love story's embrace.
Forever etched in the starry display,
Our love story written, forever to stay.

Starry-Eyed Longing

Beneath a velvet cloak of endless night,
I stand alone, bathed in moon's pale light.
The stars above, like diamonds they gleam,
Reflecting a love, a distant dream.
The wind whispers secrets, on the cosmic breeze,
Of a love once cherished, brought down to its knees.
The constellations, like celestial tears,
Mirror the longing, that silences my fears.
Will love ever return, under this starry dome?
Will I find solace, far away from home?
In this night's embrace, with a heart that yearns,
I search for answers, as the universe burns.

Starry-Eyed Hope

Beneath a canopy, vast and starlit deep,
A flicker of hope, my weary soul does keep.
The stars like diamonds, scattered and bright,
Reflect the resilience, that burns ever so light.
The moonbeams cascade, a gentle, calming flow,
Washing away doubts, helping my spirit grow.
The constellations whisper secrets untold,
A love story waiting, braver and bold.
In this starry haven, I find my reprieve,
The universe conspires, for my heart to believe.
With every twinkling star, a promise takes flight,
A love story waiting, bathed in Milky Way's light.

Celestial Euphony

Beneath a symphony of celestial might,
We dance in a waltz, bathed in moon's soft light.
The stars above, like celestial choirs,
Sing a love song, igniting our desires.
The planets align, in a cosmic decree,
Our love story written, for all the world to see.
The shooting stars, like fiery applause,
Celebrate our passion, defying all laws.
In this cosmic ballet, our souls take flight,
Two hearts entwined, forever in the light.
The universe echoes with love's sweet refrain,
A celestial euphony, forever to remain.

Starry-Eyed Reflection

Beneath a canvas of celestial grace,
We sit in silence, reflecting on our space.
The stars above, like diamonds they gleam,
Reflecting a love, a maturing dream.
The years have flown by, like shooting stars bright,
Leaving behind memories, bathed in moon's soft light.
The constellations whisper stories untold,
Of a love story written, weathered and bold.
Hand in hand we sit, with a wisdom so deep,
A love story cherished, secrets we keep.
In this quiet moment, under the starry dome,
Our love story continues, forever our home.

Whispers of Stardust

Beneath a velvet curtain, stars ignite,
Whispers of stardust, bathed in moon's soft light.
The constellations dance, a celestial show,
Reflecting the love stories, that bloom and then grow.
Each twinkling star, a memory held dear,
A stolen kiss, a whispered word, a silent tear.
The Milky Way, a river of dreams untold,
Weaving love's tapestry, braver and bold.
In this cosmic embrace, we find our peace,
Two souls entwined, with love's gentle release.
Forever etched in stardust's gentle gleam,
Our love story whispers, a celestial dream.

Starry-Eyed Adventure

Beneath a canopy, vast and ever wide,
We embark on an adventure, hand in hand as our guide.
The stars, like celestial maps, lead the way,
To hidden wonders, bathed in Milky Way's sway.
The moon, a gentle lantern, lights our path,
As we explore the unknown, free from life's wrath.
Shooting stars streak by, wishes take flight,
Dreams shared together, bathed in starry light.
In this cosmic playground, love sets us free,
Two souls intertwined, forever meant to be.
The universe unfolds, a magical sight,
Our love story written, beneath the starry night.

A Starry Lullaby

As slumber descends on the starry expanse,
A cosmic lullaby graces our trance.
The crickets chirp, a gentle refrain,
Lulling us softly, washing away pain.
The moonbeams cascade, a silvery stream,
Guiding our dreams, a celestial dream.
In constellations, our love takes flight,
A promise of forever, bathed in starry light.
With each twinkling beat, the universe sighs,
Filling our hearts with love's gentle ties.
Wrapped in stardust's embrace, we drift away,
Two souls entwined, until the break of day.

Starry-Eyed Sanctuary

On nights when darkness falls, and shadows creep,
We seek solace beneath the stars, vast and deep.
The stars, like celestial guardians, hold us tight,
In this starry sanctuary, bathed in moon's soft light.
The fireflies flicker, like celestial fire,
Guiding our way, fueled by love's desire.
Lost in this haven, worries fade away,
As we drift to sleep, under the Milky Way.
The constellations watch, with a knowing smile,
As love's embers flicker, for a long, long while.
In this starry haven, our souls take flight,
Forever bound by love's gentle light.

About the Author

Mrigendra Bharti, born on June 29, 2004, in South Delhi, India, is a multifaceted individual recognized as the owner of Mrigendra Bharti Group InfoTech India Co. Pvt Ltd. Beyond his entrepreneurial endeavors, he is a distinguished music producer, director, and a budding writer.

Embarking on his professional journey at a young age, Mrigendra Bharti's visionary leadership has led to the establishment of several successful ventures, including Croma Music Series Entertainment, Sellbrochure, Fauget Innovative, and more.

What sets Mrigendra apart is his early initiation into the world of business. His foray into the unknown realms of entrepreneurship began during his 10th-grade years, where he delved into the music industry. This initial venture laid the foundation for subsequent achievements, showcasing his dedication and resilience.

Having honed his skills in music, Mrigendra Bharti not only demonstrated significant growth in his craft but also expanded his professional network. His passion extends beyond music, encompassing app and website development, as well as graphic design.

Fueled by his creative aspirations, Mrigendra established the Mrigendra Bharti Group, a company specializing in website and app development. Currently, he collaborates with a dedicated team, collectively working on ambitious projects that promise innovation and excellence.

Mrigendra's journey serves as an inspiration, particularly for today's students, highlighting the potential of youthful determination and the ability to transform innovative ideas into successful businesses. As he continues to make strides in various domains, Mrigendra Bharti remains a dynamic force, contributing vibrancy to the realms of business, music, and technology.

Read more at https://www.imwriter-mrigendra.rf.gd.

www.ingramcontent.com/pod-product-compliance
Lightning Source LLC
Chambersburg PA
CBHW060450160726
47992CB00003B/1156